KM7 Kicks
The fine art of playing ball

BALLACK

13

(7)
Manufacturer's
identification in the
form of a logo or
stripes.

(1) There is one star for every World Cup win (for example Brasil 5 Germany 3)　**(2)** Emblem of the national football association, depicted once on the jersey (100 qcm), shorts (50 qcm) and socks (25 qcm)　**(3)** National flag, on the right and left sleeve **(12 qcm), breast, socks and shorts (12 qcm)**　**(4)** Sponsor logos jersey (25qcm), socks and shorts (12qcm)　**(5)** The player's number, on the front of the jersey, height of the number 10-15 cm, on the back of the jersey 25-35 cm, shorts 10-15 cm **(6)** The player's name on the back of the jersey (obligatory after the group stage), height of the lettering max. 7.5 cm

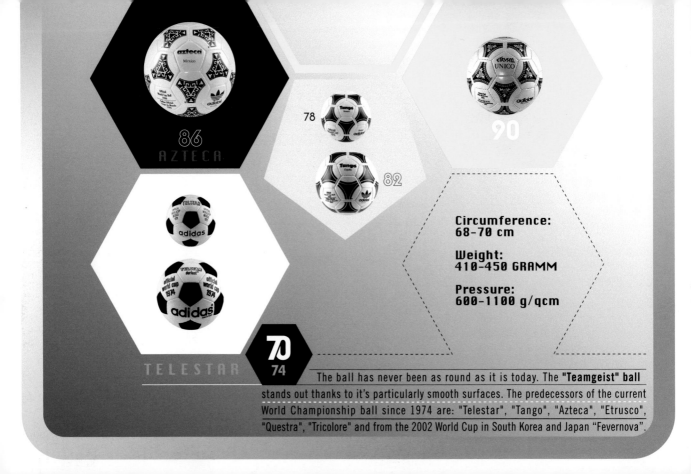

86
AZTECA

78

82

90

70
74
TELESTAR

Circumference:
68–70 cm

Weight:
410–450 GRAMM

Pressure:
600–1100 g/qcm

The ball has never been as round as it is today. The **"Teamgeist" ball** stands out thanks to it's particularly smooth surfaces. The predecessors of the current World Championship ball since 1974 are: "Telestar", "Tango", "Azteca", "Etrusco", "Questra", "Tricolore" and from the 2002 World Cup in South Korea and Japan "Fevernova".

12

PENTAGONAL PARTS

Pakistan is the world's leading football nation.

Almost every football is produced in the east of the country. But the era of the round leather football is coming to an end. Instead, balls are now being made from multi-layer laminates of polymer sheeting and cotton. Each ball consists of 20 hexagons and 12 pentagons cut and perforated in order to be sewn together with waxed threads. Subsequent coatings give the balls their striking design. This is how normal footballs are made however the current World Championship ball "Teamgeist" is being glued together using a secret process, not in Pakistan, but rather in Thailand.

Pump Me Up

Rounded segments, black and white with golden touches. Circumference: 68-70 cm. Weight 410 - 450 g. Pressure: 600 - 1100 g/cm^2 or 0.6 - 1.1 atmosphere. These standards have been specially approved for the World Championship by the world football association FIFA. Criteria: Dimensional stability, standard rebound, minimum pressure loss and minimum water absorption.

O^2

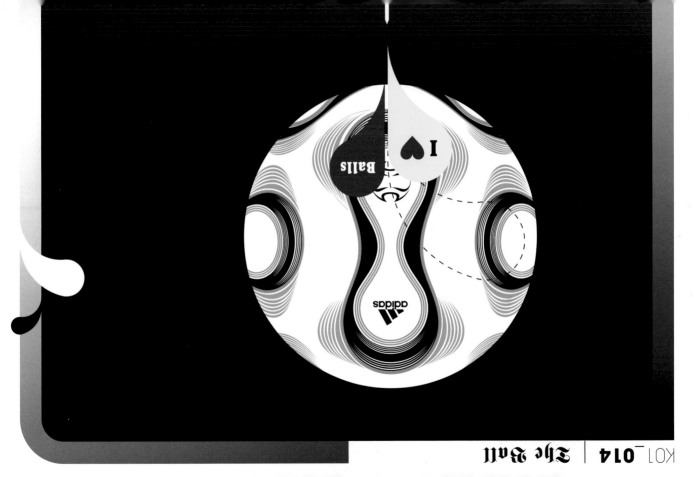

Volatile being that has to be evoked again
and again by coaches and team captains. This year the official World Championship ball is also called **"Teamgeist"** - the German word for team spirit.

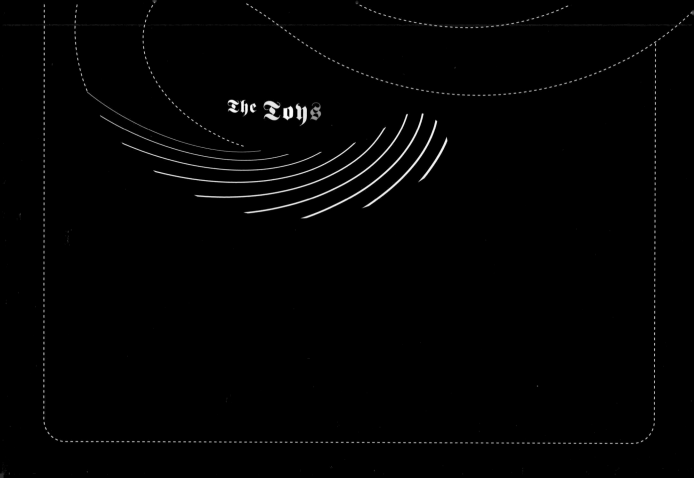

The Toys

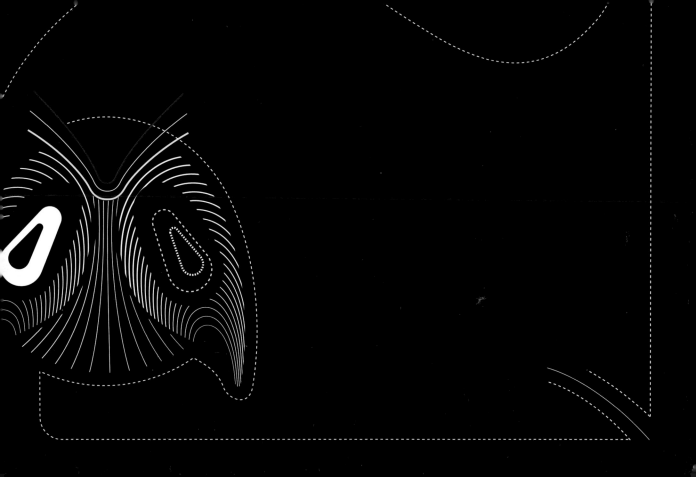

DIE VORRUNDE

DAS ACHTELFINALE: München 24.06. Leipzig 24.06. Nürnberg 25.06. Stuttgart 25.06. Kaiserslautern 26.06.

Eröffnungsspiel in München 09.06.06 (Deutschland – Costa Rica)

All stages en route to the final in Berlin.

Content:

Everything is ready.

The stadiums have all been laid out with their standardized FIFA grass rolls.
The World Championship lettering is in full bloom in city parks. We take a ride
in brand new suburban trains and drive along freshly tarred main roads
through video-monitored World Championship host cities. Some shops have
already started to sell their World Championship fan T-shirts at reduced prices.

But before the great tournament actually begins at last,

things quieten down for a brief moment among the millions of
fans in Germany. This is the moment we have been waiting for.
To welcome the principal actor of the World Championship.

We are celebrating the game of football.

In love with the ball, technically skilled and, above all,
hopelessly playful. Really looking forward to all that is to come in
Germany's stadiums in 2006.

yeah!

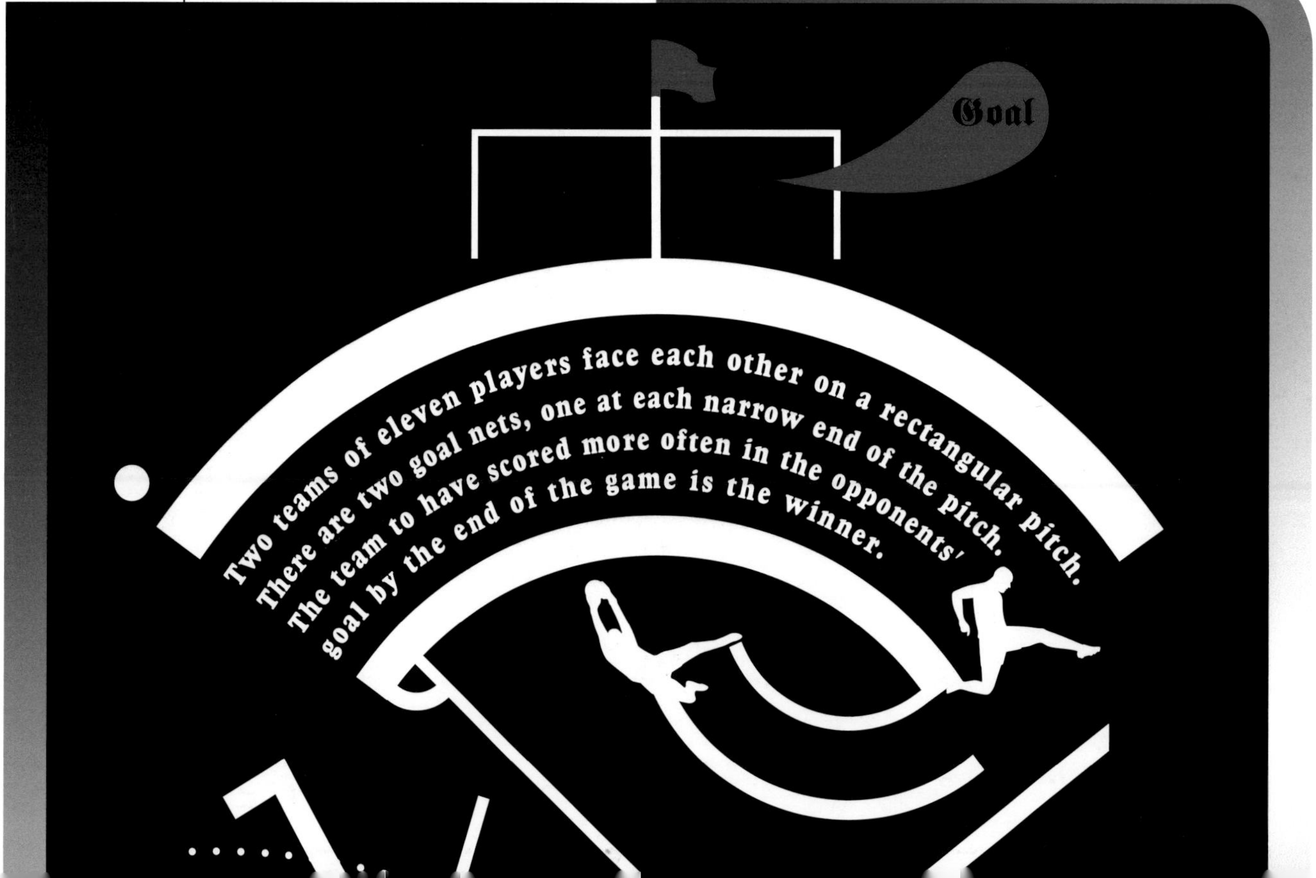

Two teams of eleven players face each other on a rectangular pitch.

There are two goal nets, one at each narrow end of the pitch.

The team to have scored more often in the opponents' goal by the end of the game is the winner.

Goal

Nike vs **Adidas**
World Cup-Final 1998 & 2002

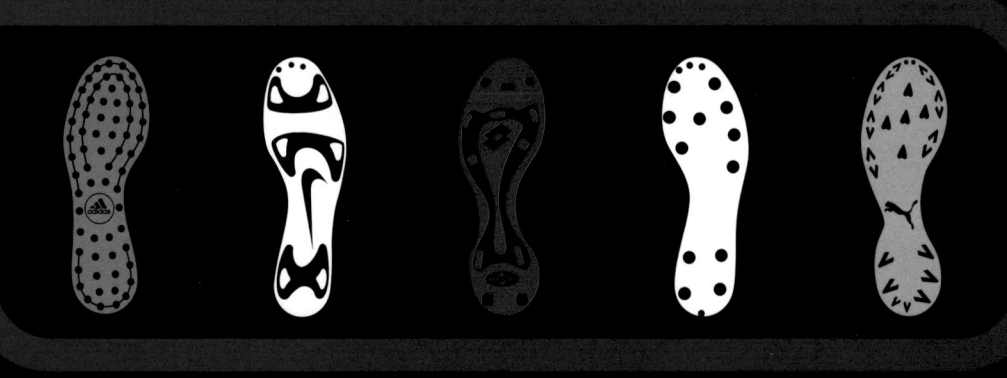

A question of profile: **Depending on the condition of the pitch, players need different kinds of studs for optimum grip.** From left to right: Multi-function fixed studs, screw studs, fixed studs, classical screw studs, arrow-shaped fixed studs.

18 mm aluminium
screw studs

The number 1 in the game often wears a padded jersey, always wears heavy-duty gloves with a non-slip rubber coating on the palm side. Goalkeepers also wear pelvic protection. A cap is worn to shade the keepers eyes from the sun.

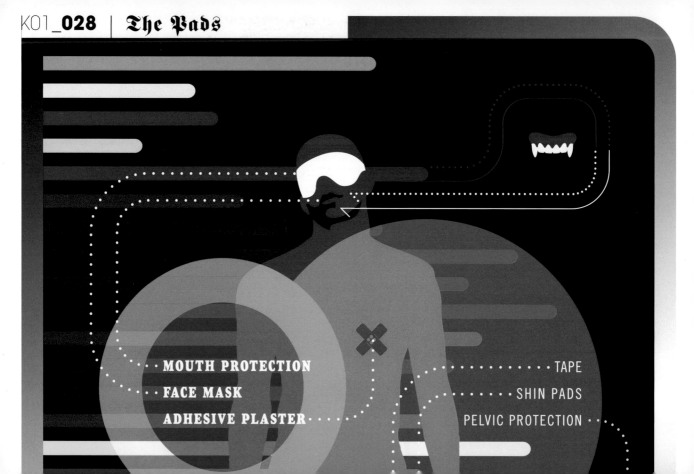

MOUTH PROTECTION

FACE MASK

ADHESIVE PLASTER

TAPE

SHIN PADS

PELVIC PROTECTION

Football is a physical sport.
Shin pads and pelvic
protection reduce the risk
of injury.
Mouth protection,
face mask, bandages
protect parts of the body
that have been injured.
Tape protects sensitive
spots.

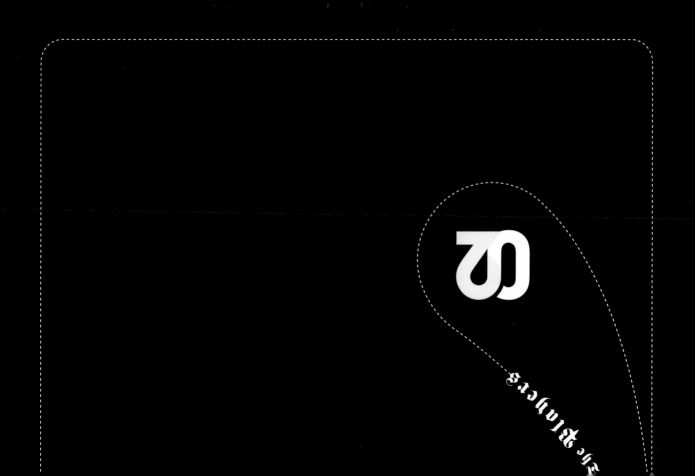

In the language of football textbooks, the player strikes the ball into the goal . . . . Shots are given different names, depending on which part of the foot actually meets the ball: . . . . instep drive, outside of the foot, inside of the foot, toe poke, back heel or full drive shot.

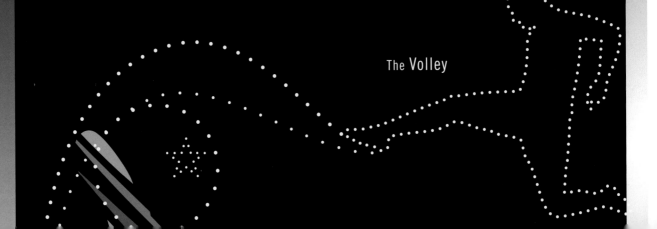

The Volley

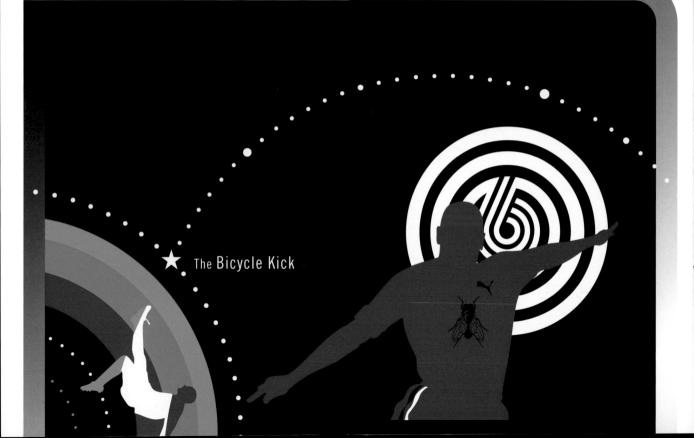

The Bicycle Kick

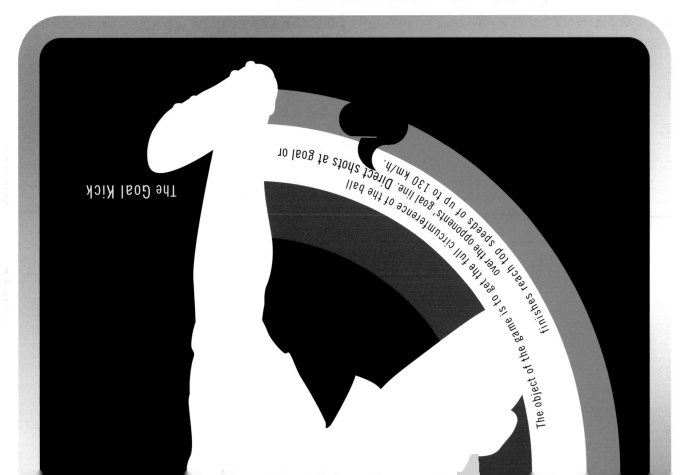

The Goal Kick

The object of the game is to get the ball over the full circumference of the opponents' goal line. Direct shots at goal or finishes reach top speeds of up to 130 km/h.

The **Goal** shy

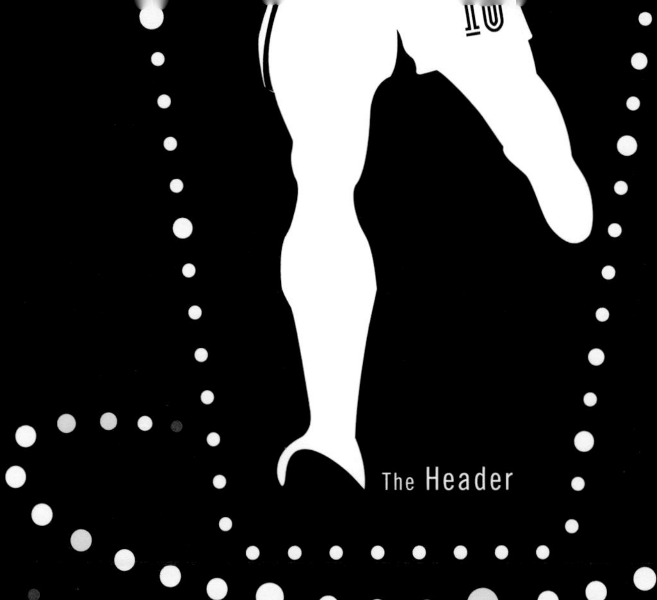

The Header

Those specialising in headers
are usually tall players who wait around in the
opponents' penalty area to nod the ball into the net from a good cross.
If they score a lot of goals, they are also called goal-getters.
Header specialists who don't manage to get their head
to even the most beautiful of crosses are
known as goal shy.

10

The Juggling

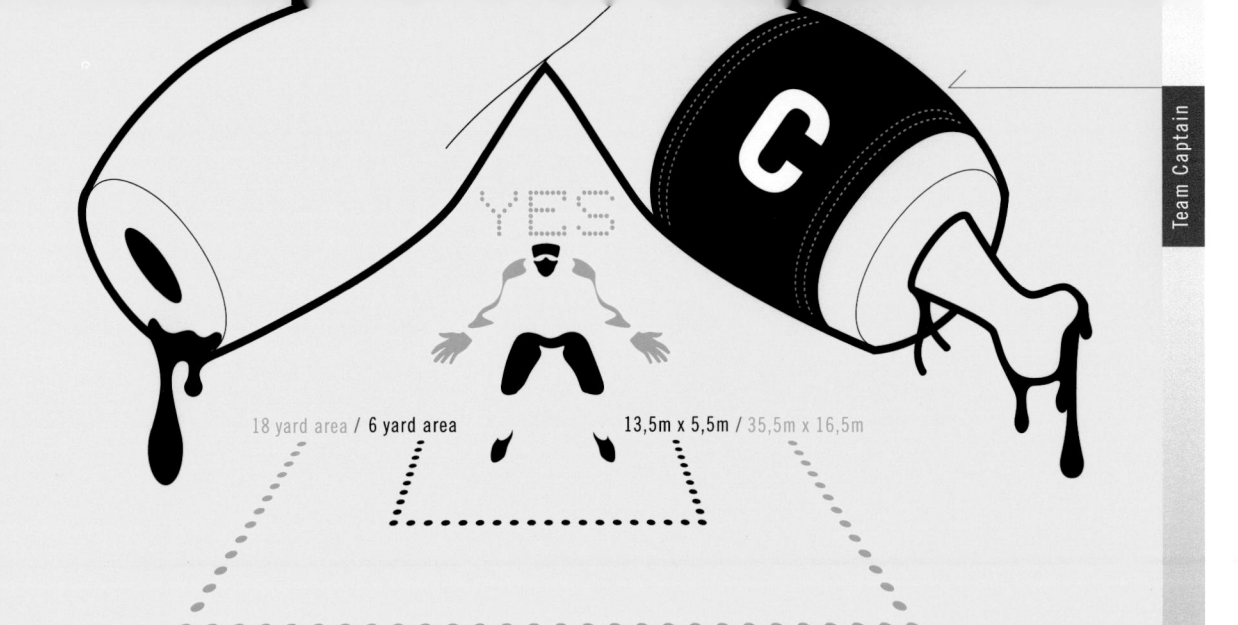

YES

18 yard area / 6 yard area   13,5m x 5,5m / 35,5m x 16,5m

N-O-! **The outfield players must not play the ball with their hand or arm.** Violations of this rule will be punished by a free kick. Handball in the player's own penalty area will even result in a penalty being given. Exceptions to this rule are unavoidable contacts between arm or hand and the ball. Such as when the ball is shot directly at a player or players are hit without being able to get out of the way.

Y-E-S-! **Goalkeepers may use their hand or arm to play the ball and may even keep hold of the ball for a short time.** But only in the 18 yard marked area around their own goal. Outside this 18 yard marked area, not even the goalkeeper can touch the ball with his hand or arm. Goalkeepers enjoy a further privilege within the 6 yard marked area. They may not be physically pressured or hindered by opposing players when trying to pick up the ball in this area.

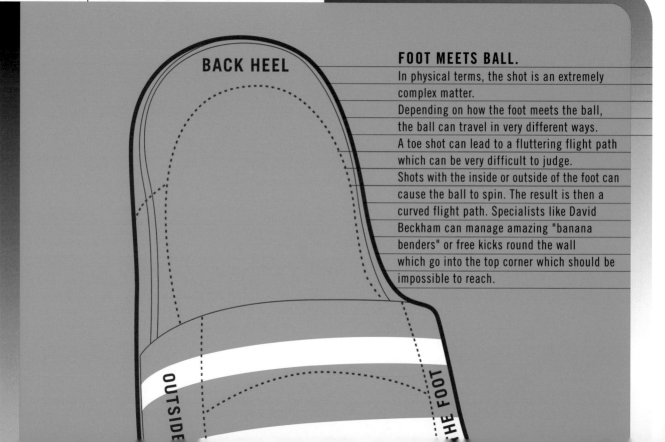

BACK HEEL

FOOT MEETS BALL.
In physical terms, the shot is an extremely complex matter.

Depending on how the foot meets the ball, the ball can travel in very different ways.

A toe shot can lead to a fluttering flight path which can be very difficult to judge.

Shots with the inside or outside of the foot can cause the ball to spin. The result is then a curved flight path. Specialists like David Beckham can manage amazing "banana benders" or free kicks round the wall which go into the top corner which should be impossible to reach.

OUTSIDE

THE FOOT

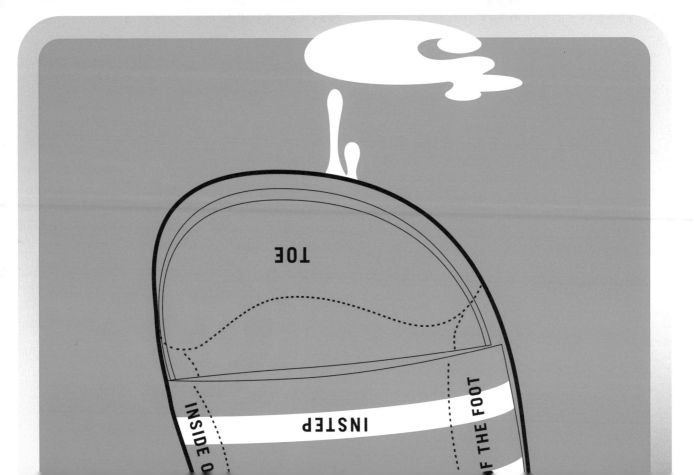

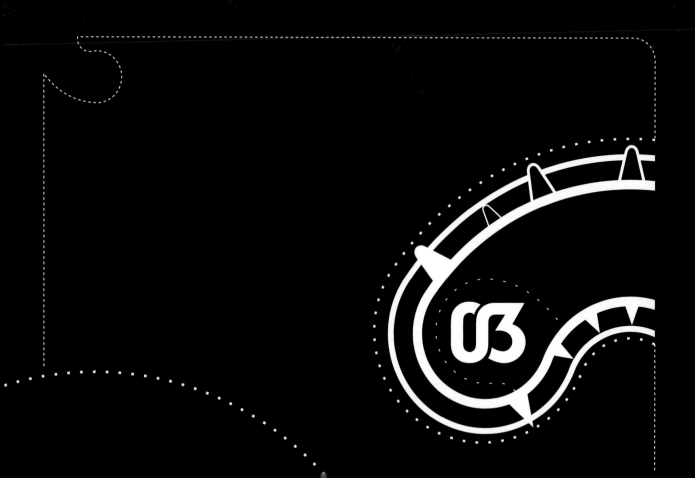

The Team

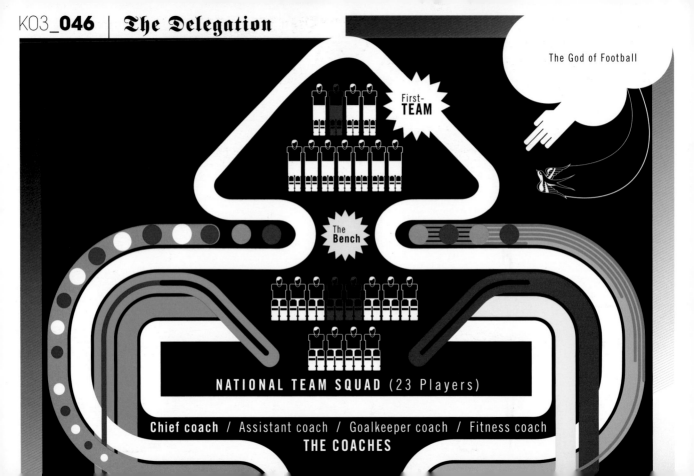

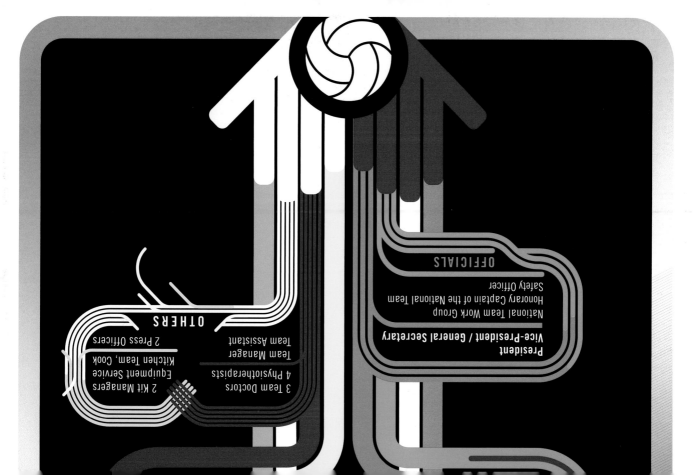

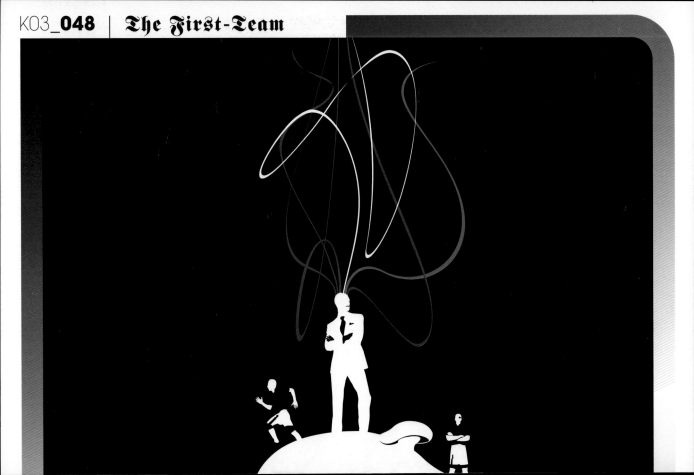

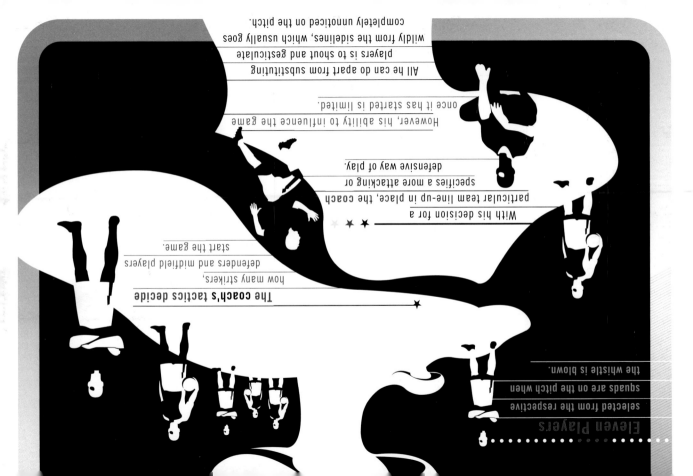

Eleven Players selected from the respective squads are on the pitch when the whistle is blown.

The coach's tactics decide how many strikers, defenders and midfield players start the game.

With his decision for a particular team line-up in place, the coach specifies a more attacking or defensive way of play.

However, his ability to influence the game once it has started is limited.

All he can do apart from substituting players is to shout and gesticulate wildly from the sidelines, which usually goes completely unnoticed on the pitch.

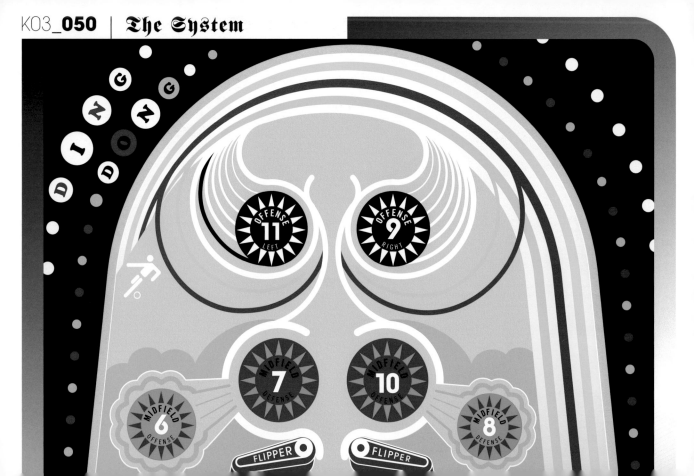

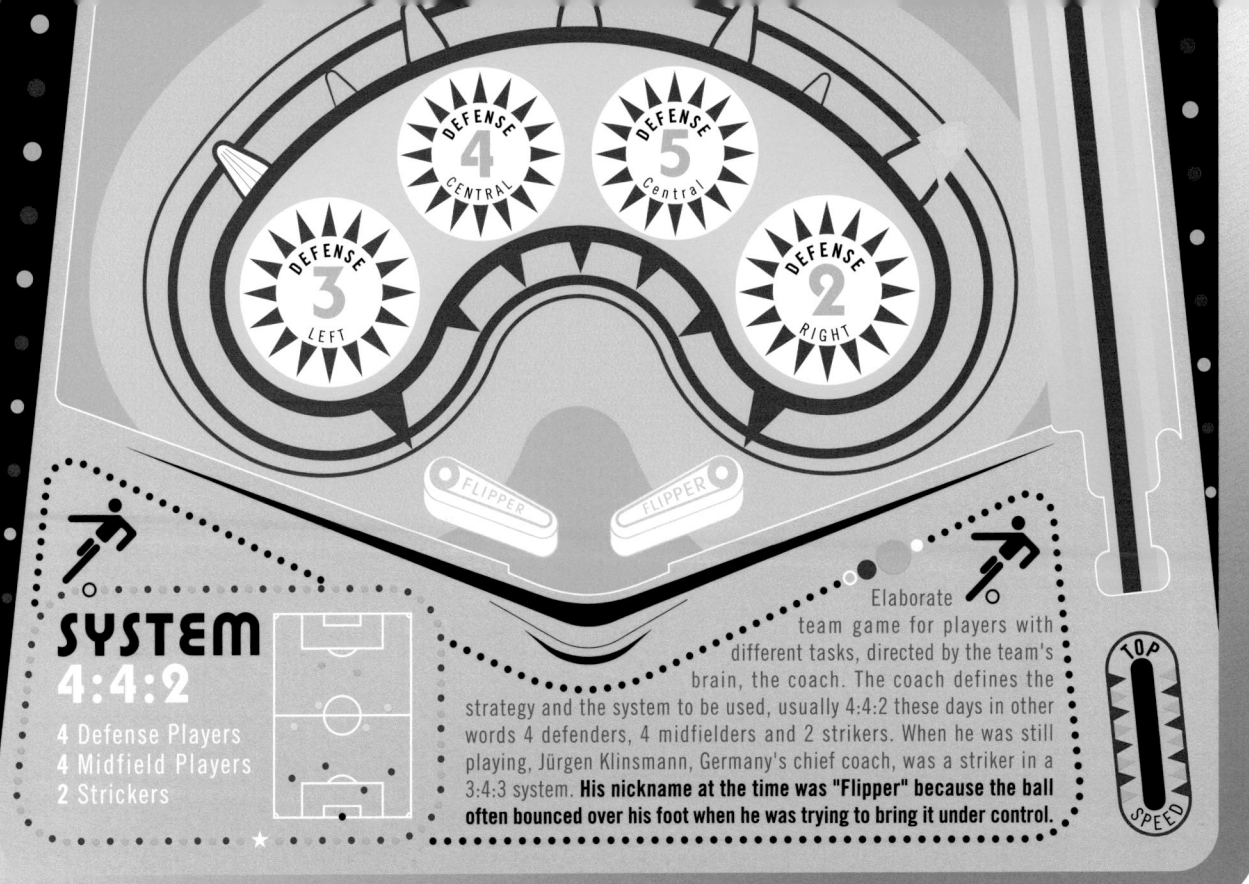

DEFENSE
4
CENTRAL

DEFENSE
5
Central

DEFENSE
3
LEFT

DEFENSE
2
RIGHT

FLIPPER FLIPPER

SYSTEM
4:4:2
4 Defense Players
4 Midfield Players
2 Strickers

TOP
SPEED

Elaborate team game for players with different tasks, directed by the team's brain, the coach. The coach defines the strategy and the system to be used, usually 4:4:2 these days in other words 4 defenders, 4 midfielders and 2 strikers. When he was still playing, Jürgen Klinsmann, Germany's chief coach, was a striker in a 3:4:3 system. **His nickname at the time was "Flipper" because the ball often bounced over his foot when he was trying to bring it under control.**

04

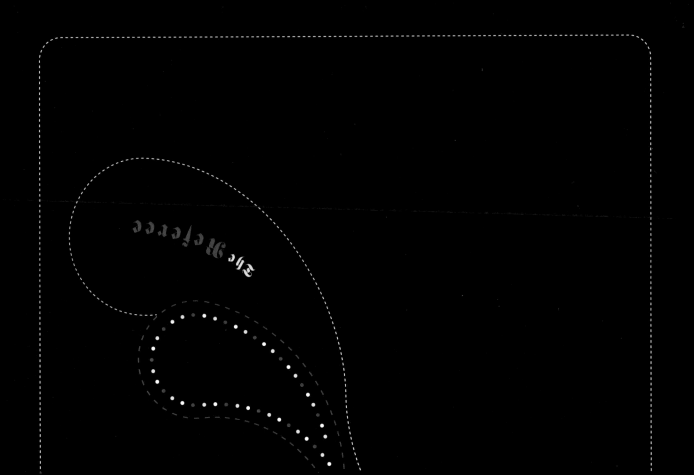

Divers are players who fall over for no apparent reason during duels for the ball and pretend to have been fouled by their opponent. This diving behaviour makes such players very unpopular with both opponents and spectators. Less due to the unsporting behaviour but more the fact that this behaviour uncovers the actual ‑ and often suppressed ‑ balance of power on the pitch. The diver tries to gain support from the most important man on the pitch: **the referee.**

If you thought players, coaches or even commercial managers were the most important figures in the game of football, you were completely wrong...

The referee is the absolute master of the pitch. He can decide the whole game with one single blow of his whistle. He brings the ball onto the pitch at the start and takes it with him again after the game has ended. He is is the real king of football, and his assistants on the right and left edges of the pitch are powerful princes.

• **Every referee will agree here,** because they know why they have decided in favour of the unpopular role of the referee. No millions in the bank, no fan clubs, but unlimited power over players and the pitch. This is much more attractive to many people than actually playing football. Particularly since it's relatively easy to start a referee's career. The minimum age is 12 years. Qualification is in the form of 20 - 50 lessons with your local football association. Apart from that, all potential referees have to do is be members of a football club and take part in regular further training events. **And before you know it, they're out on the pitch with their whistle and cards.**

THE ASSISTANT REFEREES

just like their boss, wear a black outfit. They have a flag which is equipped with an electronic sensor. If they want to draw the referee's attention to something, they can send him a vibration signal by pressing a button.

THE REFEREE

THE REFEREE – a word German reporters like to use instead of the German word to vary their commentary a little – has more equipment: **a whistle. Red card in the back pocket of his shorts. Yellow card in his breast pocket. Stopwatch. Notebook. Pen. Coin to be tossed to choose ends. Apart from the sponsor's logo, his jersey has a FIFA badge and a Fair Play logo.**

Referees and their assistants use a series of gestures
and signals specific to their profession to communicate.
The flag signals given by the assistants mean:
(1) Attention drawing e.g. for substitution (2) Corner kick
(3) Throw-in (4) Goal kick (5) Offside (6) ... in the defending third
(7) ... in the centre third (8) ... in the attacking third.

Even if many players fail to understand the referee,
his gestures are unambiguous.
Hand signals mean: (1) Caution or sending off
(2) Indirect free kick (3) Direct free kick
(4) Penalty (5) Goal kick (6) Corner kick
(7) Play on, advantage.

IN & OUT

Each team can substitute up to three players during a match. This substitution can be due to injury or for tactical reasons.

The
Medical Care

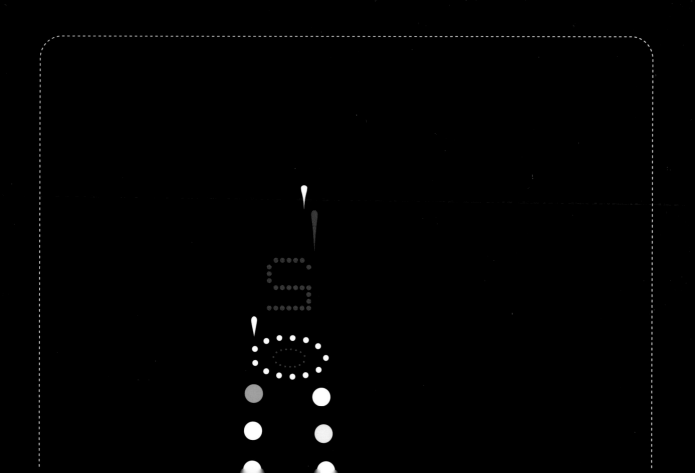

Unlikely as it is that any of the World Championship
Finalists should seek the support of a shaman
these days, there is a broad medical "no-man's land" where
methods remind us of the famous throwing of magical bones.
Lactate tests, lonely training camps, innovative nutritional products
for sports-men and joint motivation training are very helpful **if the
spiritual aspects of team leadership are also to come in useful.**

Nine tenths of footballers' bodies are made up of ligaments, tendons and cartilages.

These are stretched, overstretched or even torn off during the game but more often than not in training. This leads to players limping off the pitch to get advice from specialist orthopaedic surgeons.

The doctors' most important task now is to predict how long the player is going to be out due to the injury.

At the same time, doping tests are not a big issue in football either. If players do get caught every now and again, it's usually residual hashish or cocaine that's found in their urine. These substances are usually used to improve performance during long partying sessions rather than on the pitch, however.

Doping
is not a big issue in football.

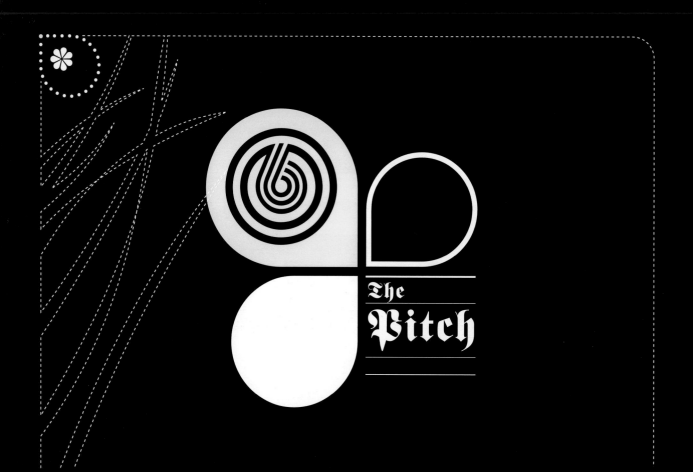

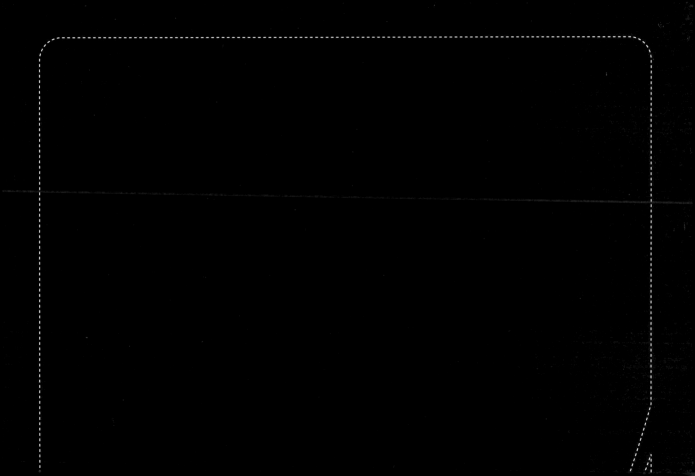

GOAL
(H) 2,4384m
(B) 7,3125m

16,4592m

5,4856m

5,4856m

16,4592m

10,9728m

Radius 0,914m

The Football Pitch:
LENGTH: 105 m, WIDTH: 68 m, 7140 qm

*

Rad. 9,144m

16-Metre-Area

Rad. 9,144m

5-Metre-Area

Unlike for national championship matches, the pitch in the stadiums chosen for the World Cup games have standardised dimensions. The funny numbers are a result of the history of the game of football. In England, the home of football, the dimensions were defined in yards. The funny numbers come from having to convert these yards into metres.

＊FRANKFURT 1974. Germany – Poland 3:1.
Water games in the Frankfurt stadium with the luckier outcome for the German team.

Chalk is still used to mark
out the lines. But the formulas
used by the pitch markers constantly evolve.
The current Line King is Uwe Nordhoff,
who looks after pitch markings
all over Europe, including nine
of the twelve German World Cup
stadiums.

LINIEN
FARBE
10L

liquid line color

Line width
10cm

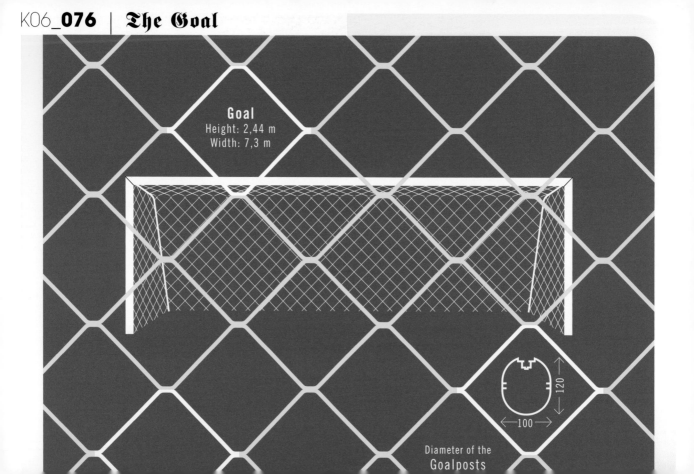

Goal
Height: 2,44 m
Width: 7,3 m

120

100

Diameter of the
Goalposts

THE GOAL. Objective of all moves. And because it is a football goal, the length of the posts and crossbar were measured in feet. The goal opening is 8 x 24 feet in size.

THE NET: A polypropylene net attached to an aluminium frame.

Net
made of Polypropylene
Mesh size:
10 x 10 cm

If players do a dance after a goal has been scored, it will be here. The quarter circle at the corner flag, around one metre in size, has seen more enraptured show dances than many an opening ceremony. At the same time, the corner flag marks the spot from which corner kicks are to be taken.

Flag min. 0,7 qm

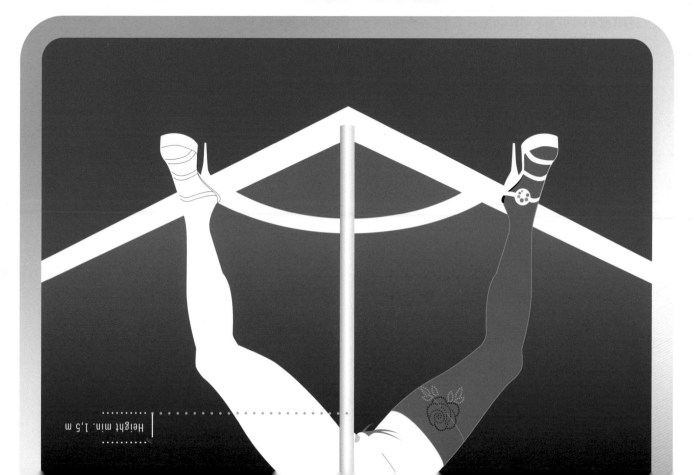

Height min. 1,5 m

Mow direction

Lolium perenne &
Poa pratensis
(Meadow panicle & Pasture grass)

Sports lawn in accordance with DIN 18035/4

The ideal World Cup grass mixture seems to have been found: **25% pasture grass and 75% meadow panicle.** Meadow panicle is a type of grass that spreads quickly horizontally and thus gives the pitch a good degree of stability.

In contrast, pasture grass grows upwards quicker, thus presenting an attractive lush-looking grass playing surface. Whereas meadow panicle is very resilient and keeps the pitch together, pasture grass recovers and grows again much more vigorously. Together they form an extremely shade and stress resilient pitch.

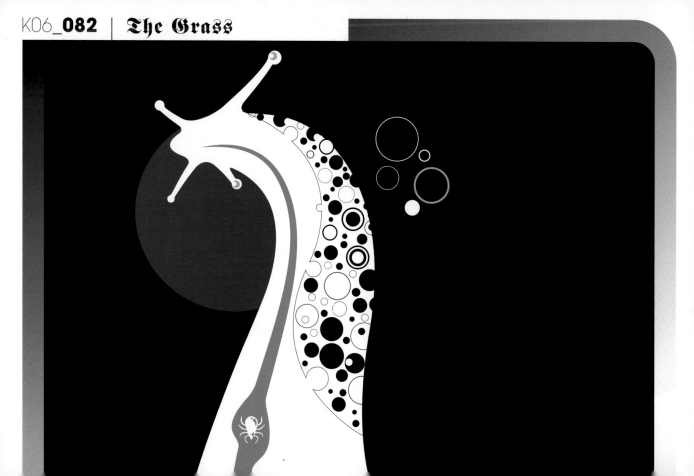

The grass rolls for the stadium pitch is pre-grown on a special substrate. Grass is sown which is extremely resilient and can survive shade. Some suppliers subject their grass rolls to stress during the initial growing phase to get the grass used to the players' studs.

18 m

1.2 m

The super roll:
333 rolls are needed
for one pitch!

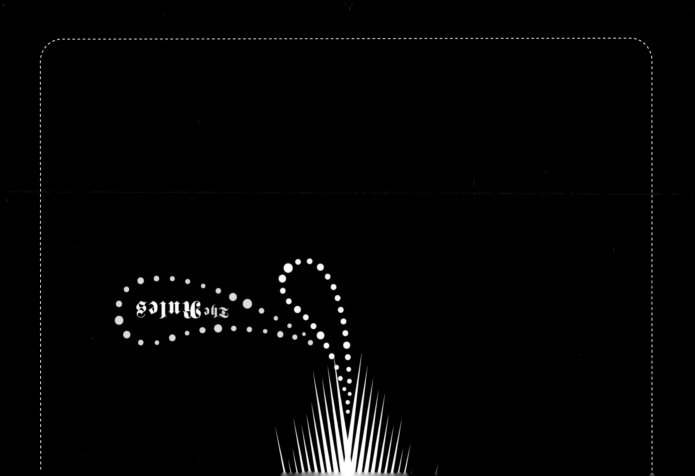

The Rules

At the beginning is the exchange of pennants.

The national anthems of both teams are played before the match. **The players swap the pennants of their football associations.** Then they choose ends. Direction of play and which team kicks off is decided by the referee and the captains of both teams at the toss of a coin.

★
★
★
★
★

A match lasts 2 halves of 45 minutes. A half-time interval of fifteen minutes (max) takes place between the two halves. Any time lost for interruptions is added to the end of the respective half. After the group stage of the World Championship tournament, any matches which are still a draw at the end of normal time will go into extra time. If neither team has won at the end of a further 2 x 15 minutes of play, the match is decided on penalties. Each coach chooses five players who take turns to shoot at the goal previously chosen by the referee. If there is still no winner, the teams take penalties in turn until one team has won.

Eleven versus Eleven

Each team has one goalkeeper and ten outfield players. The match cannot begin if one of the teams has less than seven players on the pitch. In addition to the players on the pitch, each team has twelve reserves on the bench (usually seven outside of World Championship tournaments), who may be substituted during the match. No more than three players may be substituted during one match, however. If a player is given the red card or the red/yellow card after committing an offence, he has to leave the field and his team has to finish the game with only ten men.

If a team plays the ball over the sidelines surrounding the pitch, the other team is awarded a throw-in.

If the ball is played over the line alongside the opponents goal, the opponents are awarded a goal kick, which is usually taken by the goalkeeper. If the ball is played over the line alongside the team's own goal, the opponents are awarded a corner kick which is taken from the corner flag at the side of the goal where the ball crossed the line.

If one team scores a goal, the other team is given the ball to kick off again from the centre spot, which is no consolation.

The most straightforward and relevant explanation of "offside" is: **Offside is if the linesman raises his flag and the referee blows his whistle.**
This also applies to the offside trap. If this was successful, the defenders haven't waited until the opposing strikers move offside of their own free will, they have all taken a step forward, thus leaving the opponents in an offside position.

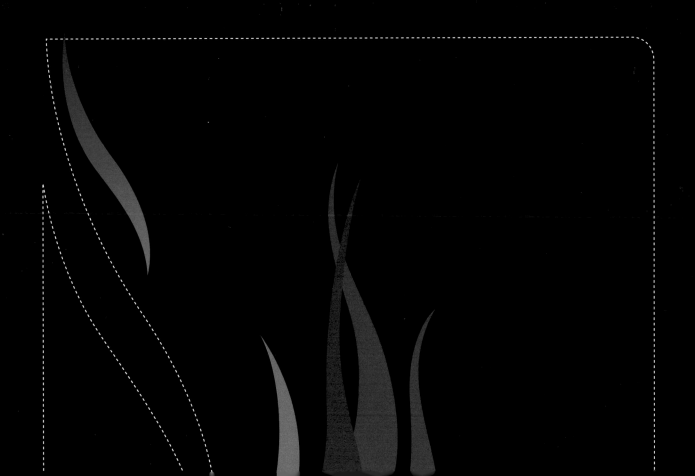

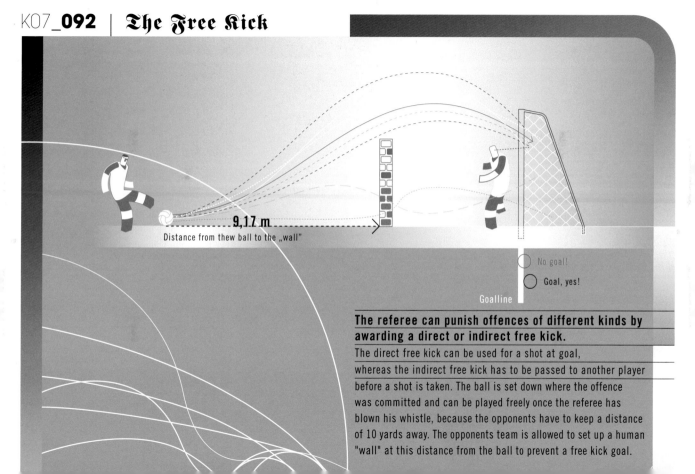

9,17 m

Distance from thew ball to the „wall"

○ No goal!

○ Goal, yes!

Goalline

The referee can punish offences of different kinds by awarding a direct or indirect free kick.

The direct free kick can be used for a shot at goal, whereas the indirect free kick has to be passed to another player before a shot is taken. The ball is set down where the offence was committed and can be played freely once the referee has blown his whistle, because the opponents have to keep a distance of 10 yards away. The opponents team is allowed to set up a human "wall" at this distance from the ball to prevent a free kick goal.

A "penalty" is one of the most severe punishments
that a referee can award. Why? **The chance of turning a penalty kick into a goal is relatively
high.** The goalkeeper has almost no chance of reaching a well-placed shot into the corner.
He would have to leap into the corner within about 0.5 seconds. And this – including reaction
time – is almost impossible.
Unless the goalkeeper decides which corner to go for and dives as the ball is struck.

PENALTY
10,97

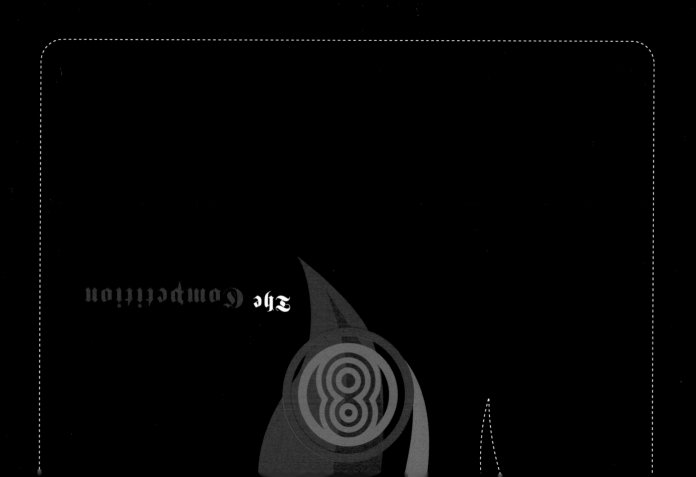

The Competition

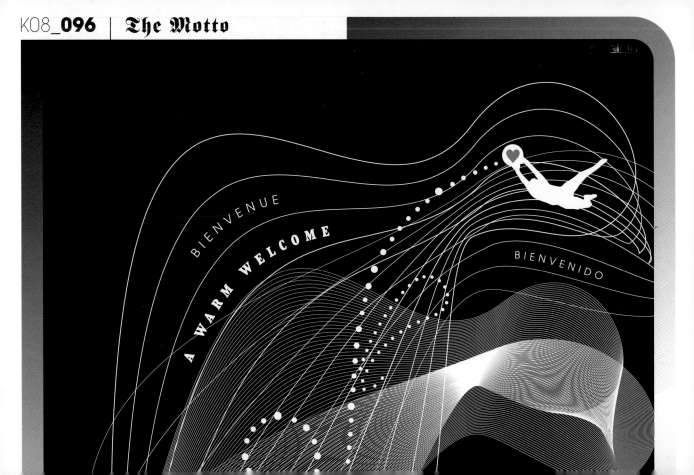

BIENVENUE

A WARM WELCOME

BIENVENIDO

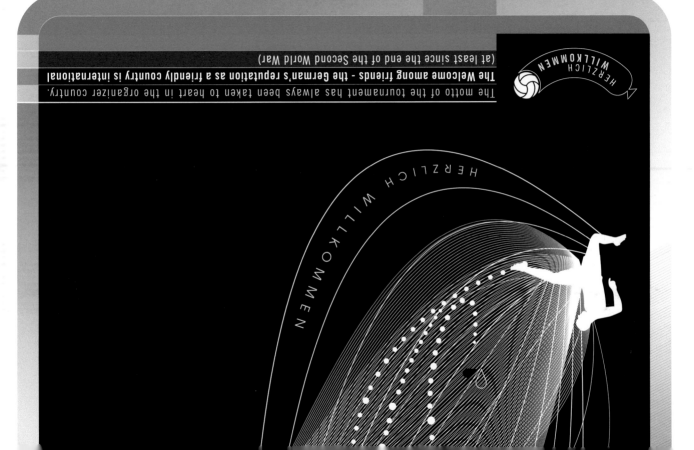

HERZLICH WILLKOMMEN

The motto of the tournament has always been taken to heart in the organizer country.
The Welcome among friends - the German's reputation as a friendly country is international
(at least since the end of the Second World War)

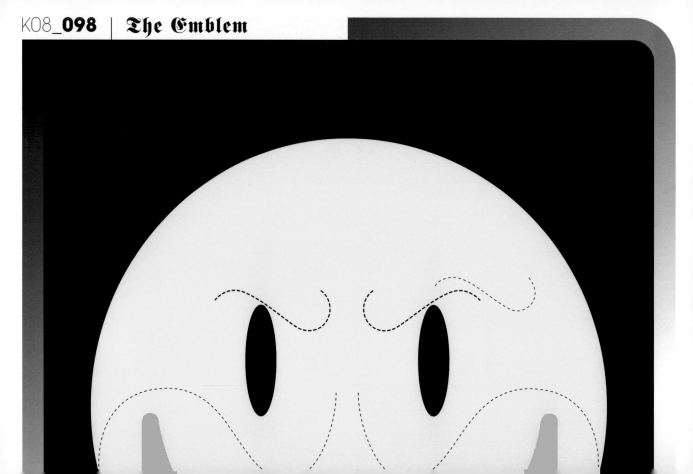

The factories producing Championship mementos are working round the clock,
with the initial pain and slog subsiding into habit.

been presented and equal horror is now directed at this:
The horror went up from artists and graphic designers alike. In the meantime, the WM mascot has also

When the official World Cup emblem was unveiled
a cry of horror

Is the World Championship emblem still showing radiant
enthusiasm or is it bawling booziness already?

There's hardly ever been anything
we've looked forward to more.

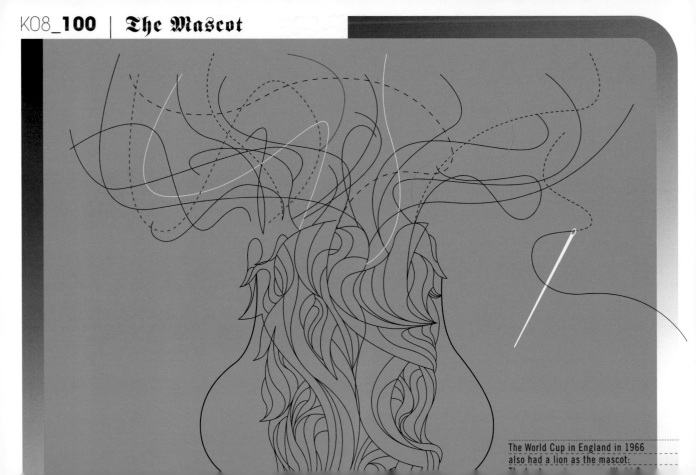

The World Cup in England in 1966
also had a lion as the mascot:

People get
used to anything.
Even a cuddly lion
2.30 metres high,
dressed in a neat football jersey
but without shorts
stumbling through
promotional events for the
World Cup.
However, to stop us
becoming too complacent,
Goleo is always accompanied by Pille.
Pille is a speaking
Football.
What won't the two of them
have to talk about?

**We already think ruefully back to the
silent footballs
accompanying previous mascots.**

1966 ENGLAND, WILLIE

1970 MEXICO, JUANITO / 1974 GERMANY, TIP & TAP
1978 ARGENTINA, GAUCHITO / 1982 SPAIN, NARANJITO
1986 MEXICO, PIQUE / 1990 ITALY, CIAO 1994 USA, STRIKER
1998 FRANCE, FOOTIX / 2002 JAPAN/KOREA REPUBLIC, SPHERIKS
2006 GERMANY, GOLEO

TIP & TAP
GERMANY

74

82

98

94

The cup is **36 cm high**, weighs **4,970 g** and is **made of** solid **18-carat gold**. It was created by the Italian sculptor Gazzaniga. The base has 2 malachite rings, one semi-precious stone and room for 17 plaques for the names of the winners — enough room to last until the World Cup 2038. The winners are allowed to keep the World Cup until the next finals and are then given a gold-plated copy.

'74 Germany

'90 Germany

'78 Argentina

1982 Italy

'94 Brazil

'98 France

'2002 Brazil

'86 Argentina

2006

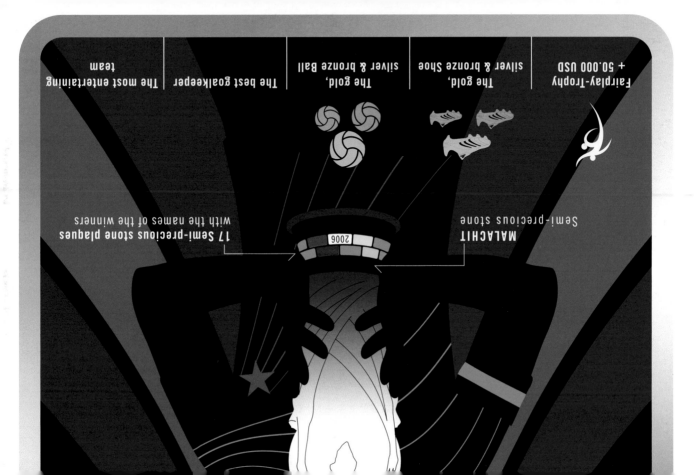

BA 728

The Participants

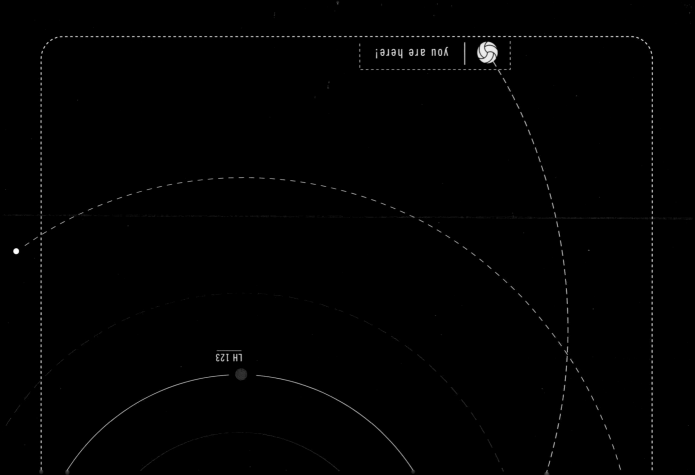

you are here!

LH 123

Globall

Before the tournament is after the tournament has begun.

Even before the official opening celebrations to the World Championship, most of the matches have already been decided. In the qualifying round for the tournament in Germany, 194 national teams completed 847 matches in front of 18 million spectators. The team from Trinidad and Tobago alone had to prove themselves in 20 matches before they were allowed to take part in their first World Championship first group match against England in Nuremberg.

On the other hand, Germany as the host nation reached the group stages without having to play a single qualifying game.

194 Teams
847 Matches
2,464 Goals

NORTH, CENTRAL AMERICAN & CARIBBEAN ZONE

EUROPEAN ZONE

ASIAN ZONE

AFRICAN ZONE

SOUTH AMERICAN ZONE

OCEANIAN ZONE

THE GAMES

WELCOME TO GERMANY

AFRICA (5 TEAMS)
ASIA (4 TEAMS)
EUROPE (14 TEAMS)
NORTH- & CENTRAL AMERICA (4 TEAMS)
SOUTH AMERICA (4 TEAMS)
OCEANIA (1 TEAM)

SOUTH AMERICAN ZONE / CONMEBOL

ARGENTINA (ARG)
BRAZIL (BRA)
ECUADOR (ECU)
PARAGUAY (PAR)

-- -- -- --

NORTH, CENTRAL AMERICAN & CARIBBEAN ZONE
CONCACAF

USA (USA)
MEXICO (MEX)
COSTA RICA (CRC)
TRINIDAD/TOBAGO (TRI)

EUROPEAN ZONE
UEFA

GERMANY (GER)
UKRAINE (UKR)
NETHERLANDS (NED)
POLAND (POL)
ENGLAND (ENG)
CROATIA (CRO)
ITALY (ITA)
PORTUGAL (POR)
SWEDEN (SWE)
SERBIA/MONTENEGRO (SCG)
FRANCE (FRA)
SPAIN (ESP)
SWITZERLAND (SUI)
CZECH REPUBLIC (CZE)

AFRICAN ZONE
CAF

ANGOLA (ANG)
COTE D'IVOIRE (CIV)
TOGO (TOG)
GHANA (GHA)
TUNISIA (TUN)

-- -- -- --

ASIAN ZONE

JAPAN (JPN)
IRAN (IRN)
KOREA REPUBLIC(KOR)
SAUDI ARABIA (KSA)

OCEANIAN ZONE

AUSTRALIA (AUS)

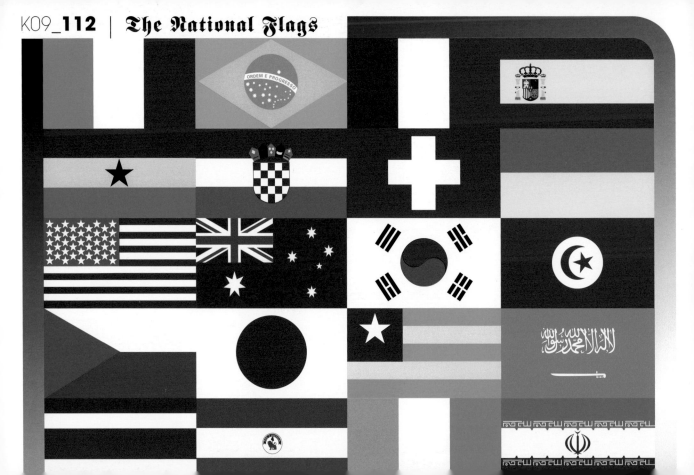

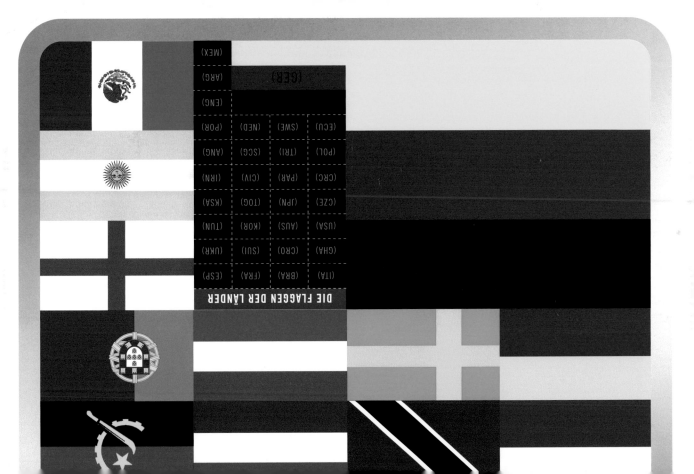

DIE FLAGGEN DER LÄNDER

(MEX)			
(ARG)	(GER)		
(ENG)			
(POR)	(NED)	(SWE)	(ECU)
(ANG)	(SCG)	(TRI)	(POL)
(IRN)	(CIV)	(PAR)	(CRC)
(KSA)	(TOG)	(JPN)	(CZE)
(TUN)	(KOR)	(AUS)	(USA)
(UKR)	(SUI)	(CRO)	(GHA)
(ESP)	(FRA)	(BRA)	(ITA)

(UKR)

(FRA)

(NED)

(SCG)

(POL)

(SWE)

(GER)

(ENG)　　(CRO)　　(ITA)　　(POR)　　(SUI)

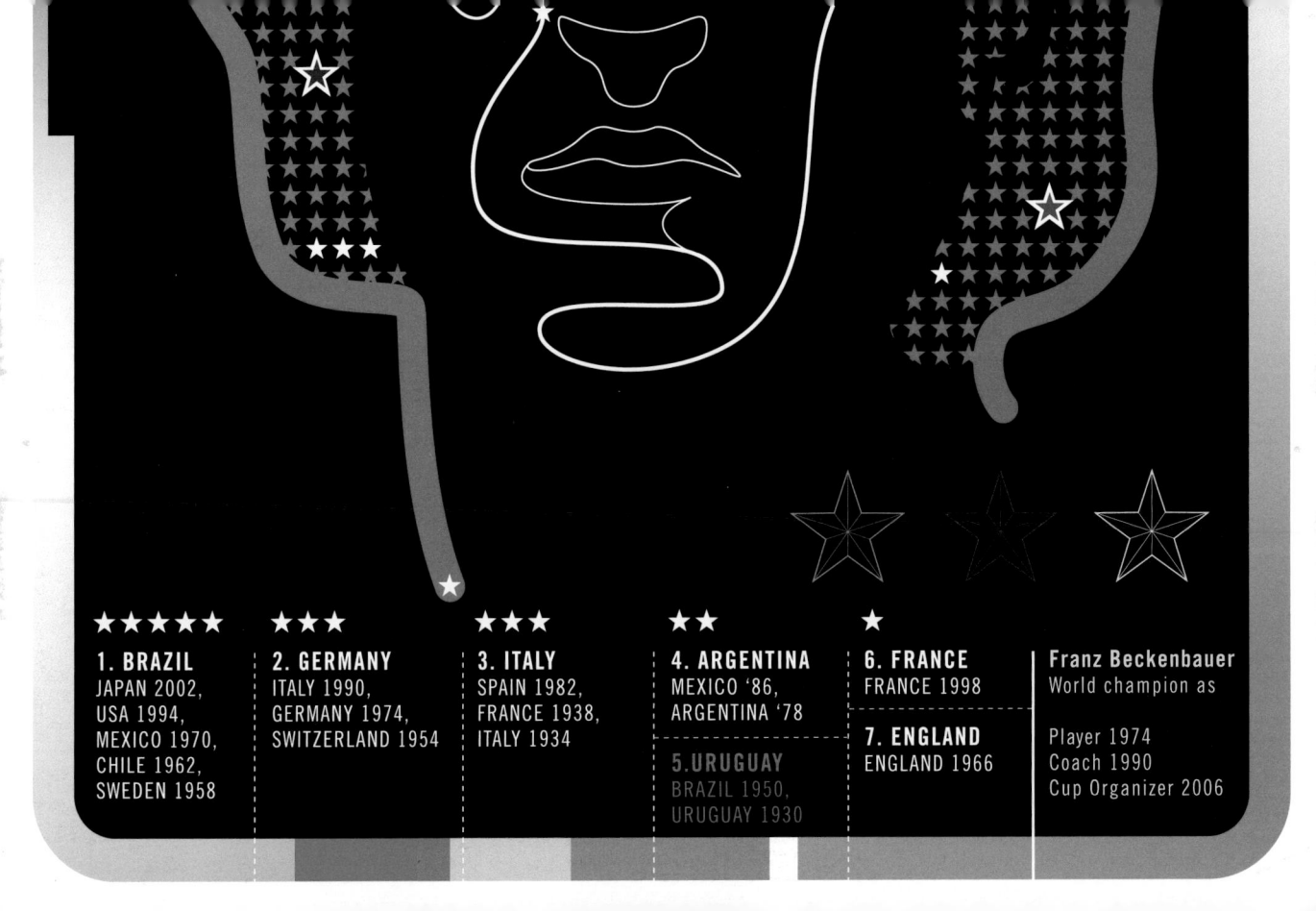

★★★★★
1. BRAZIL
JAPAN 2002,
USA 1994,
MEXICO 1970,
CHILE 1962,
SWEDEN 1958

★★★
2. GERMANY
ITALY 1990,
GERMANY 1974,
SWITZERLAND 1954

★★★
3. ITALY
SPAIN 1982,
FRANCE 1938,
ITALY 1934

★★
4. ARGENTINA
MEXICO '86,
ARGENTINA '78

5.URUGUAY
BRAZIL 1950,
URUGUAY 1930

★
6. FRANCE
FRANCE 1998

7. ENGLAND
ENGLAND 1966

Franz Beckenbauer
World champion as

Player 1974
Coach 1990
Cup Organizer 2006

Abschlag - goal kick
Abwurf - keeper's throw-out
Abseits - offside
Abseitsfalle - offside trap
Abwehr - defence
Alleingang - forward run
Angreifer - attacker
Angstgegner - bogey team
Anpfiff - kick off
Aufstellung - lineups
Anstoßpunkt - centre spot
Ausgleich - equaliser
Auswechselspieler - substitute

Ball - ball
Ballbesitz - possession
Ballverlust - to lose possession
Bananenflanke - Beckham bender
Befreiungsschlag - clearance
Beinschuss - nutmeg

Diagonalpass - crossfield pass
Direktpass - direct pass
Direktschuss - volley
Doppelpass - one-two
Dribbler - dribbler
Dropkick - half volley

Grätsche - slide tackle

Hackentrick - back-heel
Halbfinale - semi final
Halbzeit - half
Handspiel - hands
Hattrick - hat trick
Heber - lob
Heimspiel - home game
Heimvorteil - home advantage

Jubel - jubilation

Kader - squad
Kapitän - captain
Karte - card
Kopfball - header
Konter - counter-attack
Kurzpass - Short pass

Latte, Querlatte - bar, crossbar
Libero - sweeper
Linienrichter - linesman
Linksaussen - left wing

Mannschaft - team
Manndeckung - man marking

Seitenauslinie - touchline
Seitenwechsel - to swap ends
Sieg - win, victory
Sonntagsschuss - lucky shot
Spiel - match
Spieler - player
Spielfeld - pitch
Spielstand - score
Spielverzögerung - time wasting
Spielzug - move
Standfußball - pedestrian football
Steilpass - through pass
Stinkefinger - middle-finger salute
Strafraum - penalty area, box
Strafstoß verwandeln - convert the pealty
Stürmer - forward, striker

Rechtsaußen - rightwing

----

täuschen - feint
Tödlicher Pass - through ball
Tor - goal
Torjäger - goal-getter
Torlinie - goal line
Torraum - goal area, 6-yard-box
Torschiesse - score

Eck, kurzes - near post
Eckball - corner kick
Eckfahne - corner flag
Ehrentreffer - consolation goal
Eigentor - own goal
Einwurf - throw-in
Einzelaktion - solo effort
Elfer vergeben - miss from the spot
Elfmeter - penalty
Elfmeterschießen - penalty shoot-out
Endstand - final score

Fallrückzieher - overhead kick
Faustabwehr - fisted clearance
Fehlpass - poor pass
Finale - final
Flanke - Cross
Flatterball - swerving shot
Flitzer - streaker
Flugkopfball - diving header
Flügellauf - run down the wing
Flügelwechsel - wing to wing play
Flutlicht - floodlight
Foulspiel - foul
Freistoß - free kick
Führung - lead
Fussi - footie

Mauer - wall
Mittelfeldspieler - midfielder

Mittellinie - halfway line
Mittelkreis - centre circle
Mittelstürmer - centre forward

Nachspielzeit - injury time
Nachschuss - rebound
Netz - net
Niederlage - defeat / loss
Notbremse - professional foul

Pass aus dem Fußgelenk - quick flick
Pause - half time
Pfiff - whistle
Pfosten - post
Pokal - cup
Pokal gewinnen - lifting the silverware

Querpass - square pass

Rechtsaußen - rightwing

Schal - scarf
Schiedsrichter - referee
Schwalbe - dive

Torwart - goalkeeper, goalie
Trainer - coach
Trikot - jersey
Tunneln - to nutmeg

Unentschieden - remis - draw

Verlängerung - extra time
Verteidiger - defender
Viertelfinale - quarter final
Vizemeister - runners-up

Wiederanpfiff - second half kick off
Wimpel - pennant

Zweikampf - tackle

Once upon a time
there was a country that
didn't invent the game of football.

But it almost did.
The first leather ball rolled over a
German pitch as early as in October 1874.
And because we Germans do everything we do
particularly thoroughly, the first written set
of rules was published in 1875.

Germany has had the largest Football Association in the world for
many years. With an "Kaiser" as its Vice-President.

... and because everything ends well in fairytales, Germany will become
world champion of football in its own home country, Klinsmann will return to
his Swabian home to live a happy life as a high DFB functionary ever after.

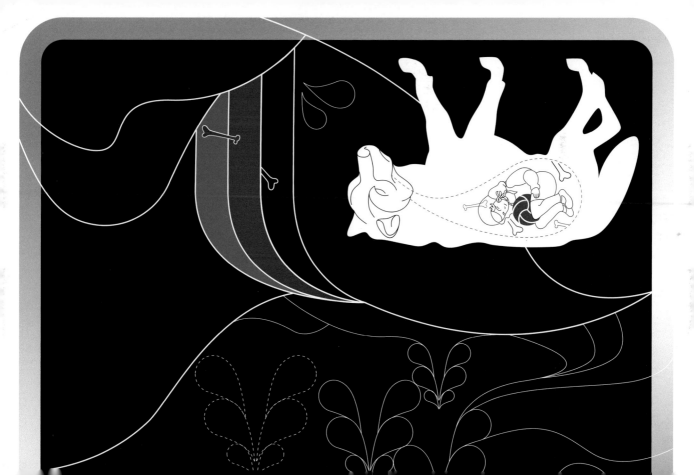

KM7 Kicks
The fine art of playing ball

Designbureau KM7
Gutzkowstraße 9
D-60594 Frankfurt/Main
Germany

Phone +49.(0)69.962181.30
mai@km7.de
www.km7.de

--- ★

Design and illustration by Klaus Mai &
Christian Bitenc (c.bitenc@t-online.de, www.bitenc.de)

Pages 140, 142, 144 146 & 148 by Sebastian Schöpsdau
(schoepsdau@vonherzenweb.de)

written by Thomas Heise (heise@open-agentur.de)

-- ★

Edited by Robert Klanten

Published by Die Gestalten Verlag, Berlin
ISBN 10: 3-89955-169-9
ISBN 13: 978-3-89955-169-3

-- ★ ---

Bibliographic information published
by Die Deutsche Bibliothek
Die Deutsche Bibliothek lists this publication in the
Deutsche Nationalbibliografie; detailed bibliographic data
are available in the Internet at http://dnb.ddb.de.

For more information please check:
www.die-gestalten.de

Respect copyright, encourage creativity

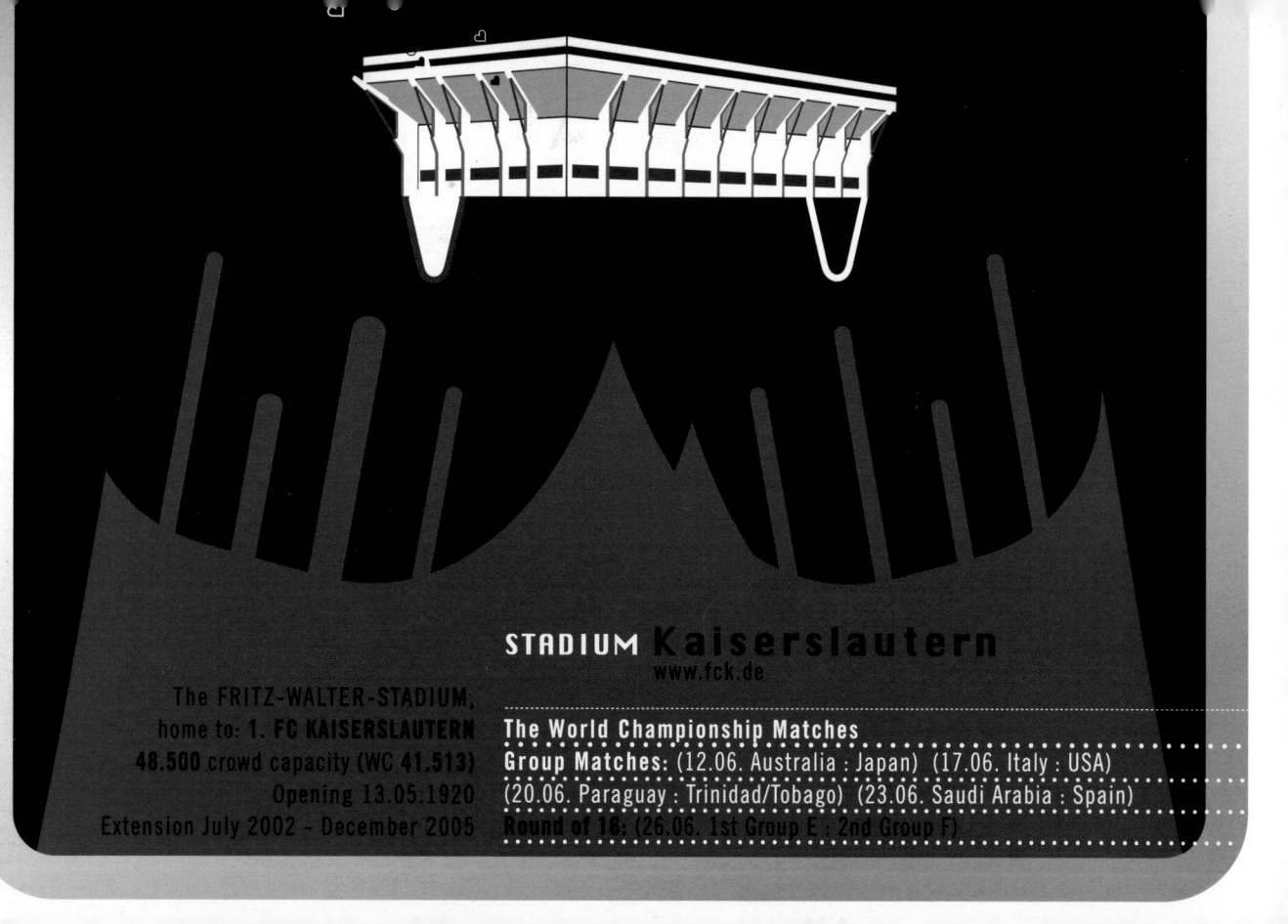

STADIUM **Kaiserslautern**
www.fck.de

The FRITZ-WALTER-STADIUM,
home to: **1. FC KAISERSLAUTERN**
48.500 crowd capacity (WC **41.513**)
Opening 13.05.1920
Extension July 2002 - December 2005

The World Championship Matches
Group Matches: (12.06. Australia : Japan) (17.06. Italy : USA)
(20.06. Paraguay : Trinidad/Tobago) (23.06. Saudi Arabia : Spain)
Round of 16: (26.06. 1st Group E : 2nd Group F)

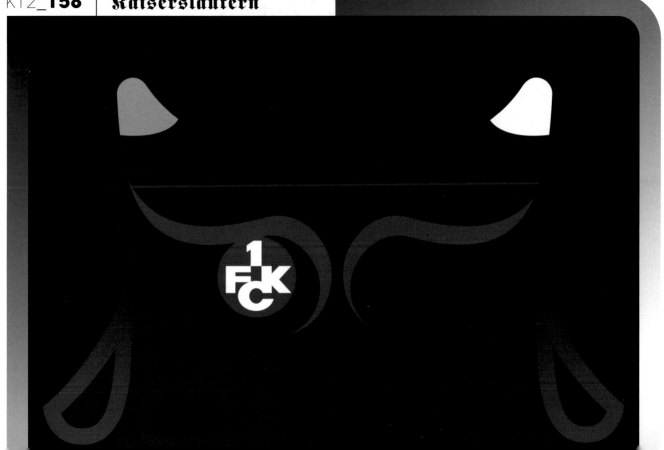

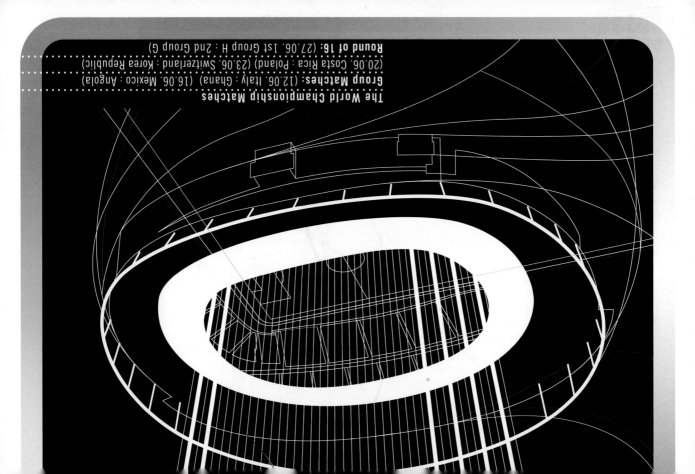

The World Championship Matches

Group Matches: (12.06. Italy : Ghana) (16.06. Mexico : Angola)
(20.06. Costa Rica : Poland) (23.06. Switzerland : Korea Republic)
Round of 16: (27.06. 1st Group H : 2nd Group G)

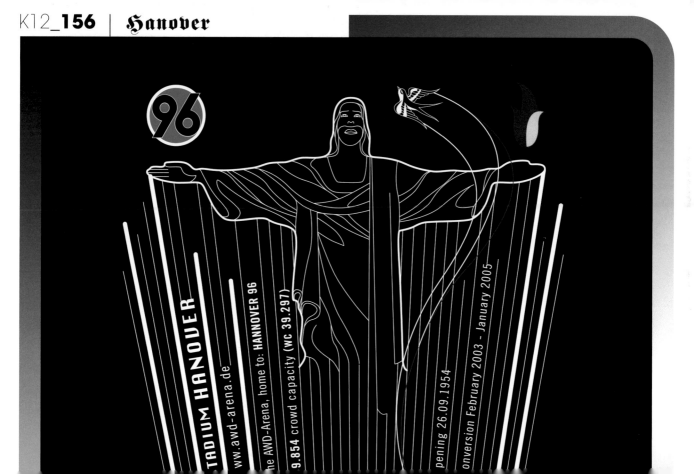

The OLYMPIASTADION, home to:
HERTHA BSC

74.220 crowd capacity **(WC 66.021)**
Opening 01.08.1936
Conversion July 2000 - December 2004

The World Championship Matches
Group Matches: (13.06. Brazil : Croatia) (15.06. Sweden : Paraguay)
(20.06. Ecuador : Germany) (23.06. Ukraine : Tunisia)
Quarter Final: (30.06. Winner LS Match 1 : Winner LS Match 2)
FINAL: (09.07. Winner 1st Semi Final : Winner 2nd Semi Final)

STADIUM BERLIN
www.olympiastadion-berlin.de

HERTHA BSC
HerthaBSC
BERLIN

Quarter Final: (01.07.) Winner IS Match 1 : Winner IS Match 2 (13.06. Korea Republic : Togo) (17.06. Portugal : Iran) (21.06. Netherlands : Argentina) **Group Matches:** (10.06. England : Paraguay) Opening 21.05.1925, Conversion 2002 – 2005 **The World Championship Matches, Group Matches (WC 43.324)** The COMMERZBANK-ARENA, home to: **EINTRACHT FRANKFURT** 52.300 crowd capacity

STADIUM MUNICH

www.allianz-arena.de

The ALLIANZ-ARENA, home to:
FC BAYERN MÜNCHEN &
TSV MÜNCHEN 1860

66.000 crowd capacity (WC **59.416**),
Opening 30.05.2005

The World Championship Matches
Opening Match 09.06.05 Germany - Costa Rica
more Group Matches: (14.06. Tunisia : Saudi Arabia)
(18.06. Brazil : Australia) (21.06. Cote d'Ivoire : Serbia/Montenegro)
Round of 16: (28.06. 1st Group A - 2nd Group B)
2nd Semi Final: (05.07. Winner Qf Match 3 - Winner Qf Match 4)

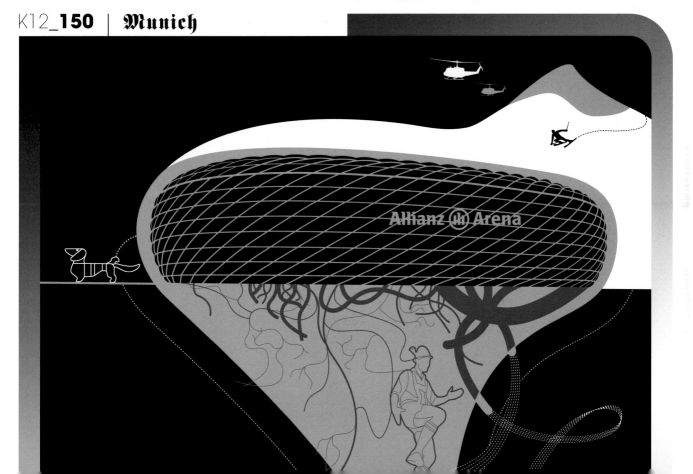

The World Championship Matches

Group Matches:
(11.06 Mexico : Iran)
(15.06 England : Trinidad/Tobago)
(18.06 Japan : Croatia)
(22.06 Ghana : USA)

Round of 16:
(25.06 1st Group D : 2nd Group C)

STADIUM NUREMBERG

www.easycredit-stadion.de

The EASYCREDIT Stadium, home to:

1. FC NÜRNBERG

46.780 crowd capacity (WC 36.898)

Opening 10.06.28

The RheinEnergieStadion, home to:
1. FC Köln
50.374 crowd capacity (WC 40.490)
Opening 16. März 1923
Conversion January 2002 - July 2004

The World Championship Matches
Group Matches:
(11.06. Angola : Portugal)
(17.06. Czech Republic : Ghana)
Sweden : England)
Round of 16:
(26.06. 1st Group G : 2nd Group H)

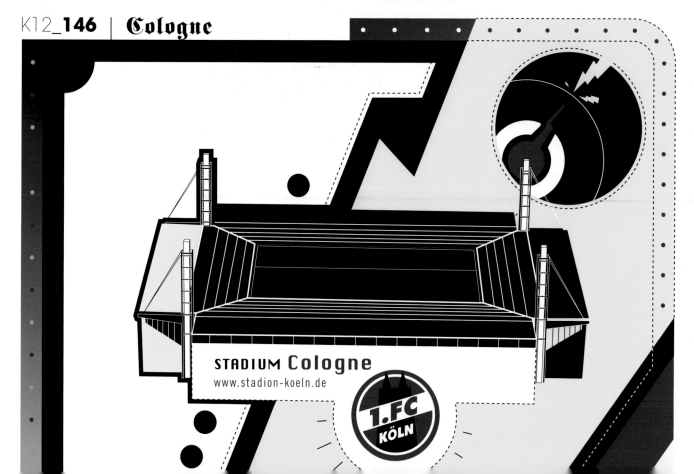

STADIUM Cologne
www.stadion-koeln.de

The World Championship Matches
Group Matches

Group Matches:
(10.06. Argentina : Cote d'Ivoire)
(15.06. Ecuador : Costa Rica)
(19.06. Saudi Arabia : Ukraine)
(22.06. Czech Republic : Italy)
Quarter Final:
(30.06. Winner LS Match 5 : Winner LS Match 6)

The AOL-Arena, home to:
Hamburger SV
55.800 crowd capacity
(WC 45.442)
Opening 13. 09. 1925
Conversion 1999

The World Championship Matches:

Group Matches:
(11.06: Serbia/Montenegro : Netherlands)
(14.06: Spain : Ukraine)
(18.06: France : Korea Republic); (21.06: Iran : Angola)
Round of 16: (24.06, 1st Group C : 2nd Group D)

FC SACHSEN LEIPZI

44.345 crowd capacity

Opening 1956, conversion 2...

The ZENTRALSTA...

STADIUM DORTMUND

www.bvb.de

The World Championship Matches:

Group Matches

(10.06. Trinidad/Tobago : Sweden)
(14.06. Germany : Poland)
(19.06. Togo : Schwitzerland)
(22.06. Japan : Brazil)

Round of 16:

(27.06. 1st Group F : 2nd Group E)

Semi Final:

(04.07. Winner Of Match 1 : Winner Of Match 2)

The Signal Iduna Park, home to:

BVB 09 Dortmund

81.264 crowd capacity

(WC 60.285)

Opening 02. April '74

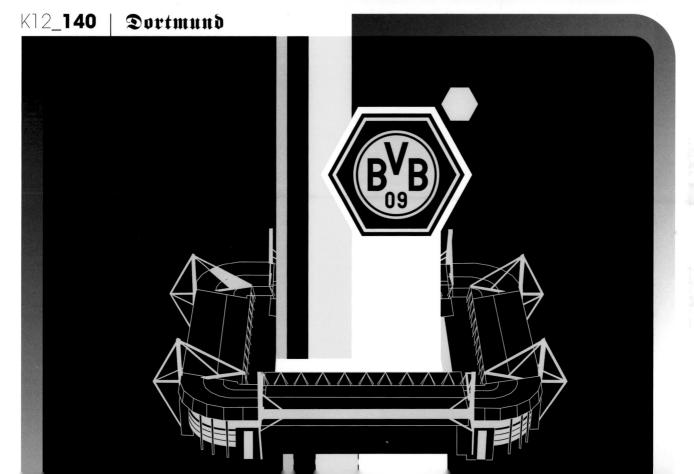

STADIUM STUTTGART
www.gottlieb-daimler-stadion.de

57.000 crowd capacity (WC 47.757), Opening 23.07.33
The GOTTLIEB-DAIMLER-STADION, home to: **VFB STUTTGART**

The World Championship Matches
Group Matches: (13.06. France : Switzerland),
(16.06. Netherlands : Cote d'Ivoire),
(19.06. Spain : Tunisia), (22.06. Croatia : Australia)

Round of 16: 25.06. (1st Group B : 2nd Group A)
THIRD-PLACE PLAY-OFF: 08.07. (Loser 1st Semi Final :
Loser 2nd Semi Final)

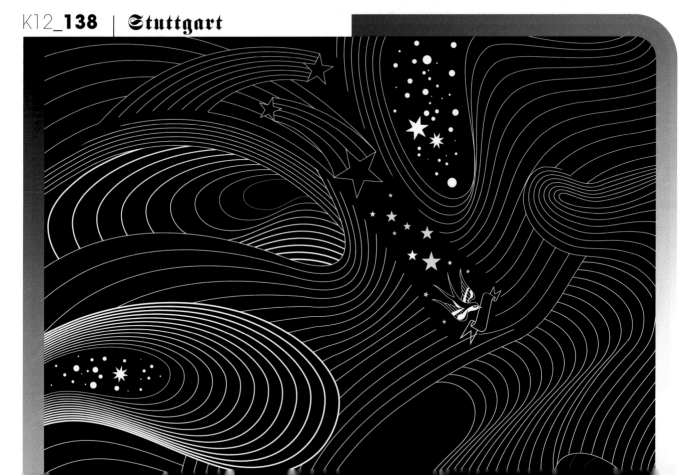

The VELTINS ARENA
Home to:
FC SCHALKE 04

World Championship Matches
GROUP MATCHES: (09.06. Poland : Ecuador) (12.06. USA : Czech Republic)
(16.06. Argentina : Serbia/Montenegro) (21.06. Portugal : Mexico)
QUARTER FINALE: (01.07. Winner LS Match 3 : Winner LS Match 4)

61.524 crowd capacity
(WC **48.426**)
Opening 13.08.01

STADIUM
GELSENKIRCHEN
www.veltins-arena.de

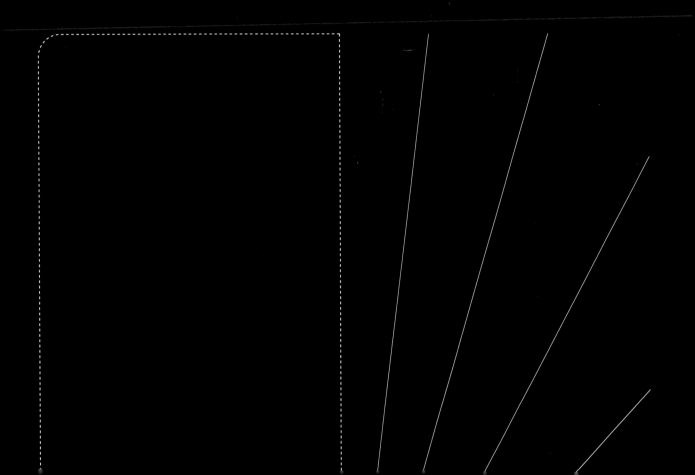

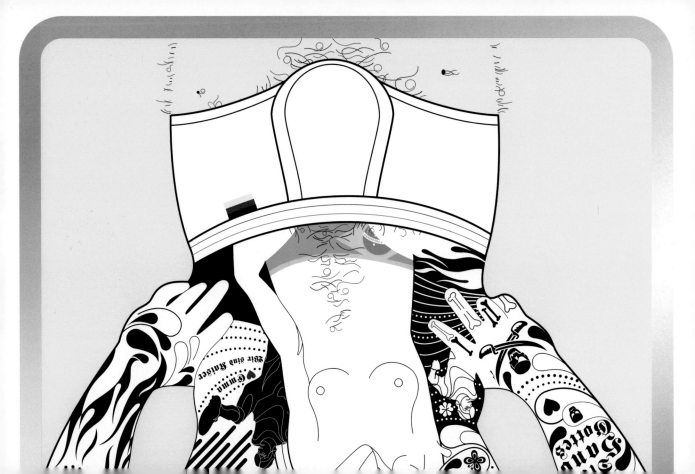

The Berlin wall.

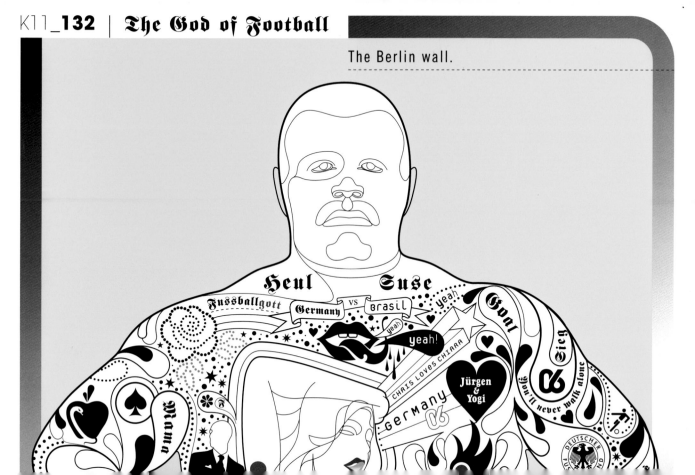

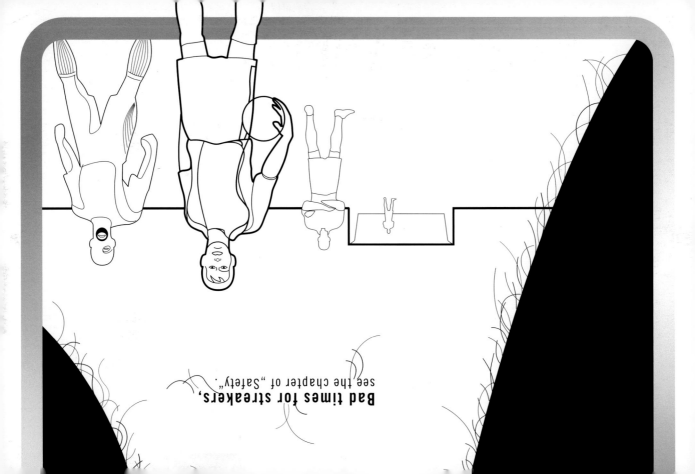

Bad times for streakers,
see the chapter of „Safety".

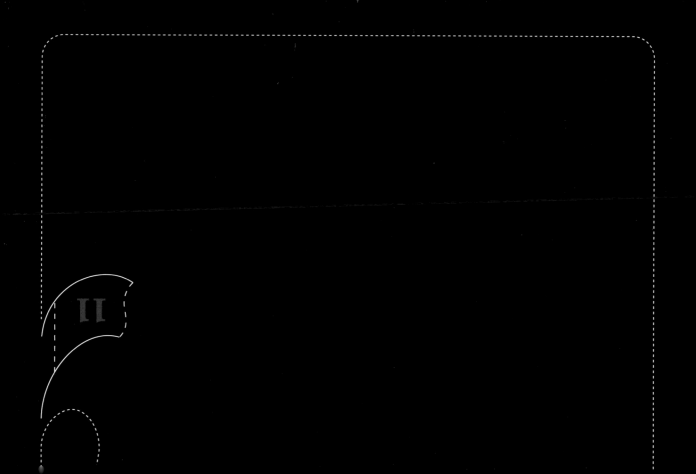

II

It now looks as though the German Army will not be called in to safeguard the World Cup. Nevertheless, we will experience a record-breaking amount of security forces. Dramatic meetings between fans are thus more likely to take place in the streets and pubs than in and around the stadiums.